D1261129

The Southern Haunting of

Truman Capote

Also by Marie Rudisill

- *Truman Capote: The Story of His Bizarre and Exotic Boyhood* (with James C. Simmons)
- *Sook's Cookbook: Memories and Traditional Receipts from the Deep South*
- *Critter Cakes & Frog Tea: Tales and Treats from the Emerald River*

Also by James C. Simmons

- *The Novelist as Historian: Essays on the Victorian Historical Novel*
- *Truman Capote: The Story of His Bizarre and Exotic Boyhood* (with Marie Rudisill)
- *The Secrets Men Keep* (with Ken Druck)
- *Passionate Pilgrims: English Travelers to the World of the Desert Arabs*
- *The Big Book of Adventure Travel*
- *Americans: The View from Abroad*
- *Castaway in Paradise: The Incredible Adventures of True-Life Robinson Crusoes*
- *Star-Spangled Eden: 19th Century America Through the Eyes of Dickens, Wilde, Frances Trollope, Frank Harris, and Other British Travelers*

The Southern Haunting of
Truman Capote

Marie Rudisill

with **James C. Simmons**

Cumberland House
Nashville, Tennessee

© 2000 by Marie Rudisill and James C. Simmons

Published by Cumberland House Publishing, Inc., 431 Harding
Industrial Drive, Nashville, TN 37211

Cover design: Unlikely Suburban Design
Text design: Mary Sanford

Library of Congress Cataloging-in-Publication Data
Rudisill, Marie.
    The Southern haunting of Truman Capote / Marie Rudisill with
James C. Simmons.
        p. cm.
    ISBN 1-58182-136-0 (alk. paper)
    1. Capote, Truman, 1924---Homes and haunts--Alabama--
Monroeville. 2. Authors, American--20th century--Family relation-
ships. 3. Capote, Truman, 1924---Childhood and youth. 4. Authors,
American--20th century--Biography. 5. Monroeville (Ala.)--Social
life and customs. 6. Capote, Truman, 1924---Family. 7. Southern
States--In literature. 8. Monroeville (Ala.)--Biography. 9. Rudisill,
Marie. I. Simmons, James C. II. Title.

PS3505.A59 Z867 2000
813'.54--dc21

                                                    00-043087

Printed in the United States of America
1 2 3 4 5 6 7—05 04 03 02 01 00

For my son, Jim Rudisill, and his family;
Karen, Sandy, Candy, and Mike Rudisill

—*Marie Rudisill*

+⌒+ +⌒+ +⌒+

For Ed and Edie Drcar

—*James C. Simmons*

Contents

Acknowledgments   11

Prologue   13

1   Monroeville, Alabama: Jenny's House   41

2   A Christmas Memory   63

3   The Grass Harp   81

4   Children on Their Birthdays   97

5   Other Voices, Other Rooms   111

Epilogue   133

Acknowledgments

The concept for this book originated with the late Joe Fox, Truman Capote's editor at Random House for over twenty years. We became friendly after Truman's death, chatting on the telephone and engaging in an exchange of letters. On several occasions I sent him boxes of delicious grapefruit harvested from the trees in my backyard here in Hudson, Florida. Ten years after Truman's death, Mr. Fox suggested that I write a short book "of a length between *A Christmas Memory* and *The Grass Harp* which would treat the Southern origins of some of your nephew's most popular early works." He thought that such a book would be "utterly unlike anything else written on Truman and would do well." We had an exchange of correspondence on the idea shortly before Mr. Fox's death. The result of his suggestion is the present volume.

Marie Rudisill

Prologue

Truman's Death:
August 25, 1984

I was watching the eleven o'clock news on CBS on that memorable night of August 25, 1984, when a bulletin suddenly appeared on the screen. "TRUMAN CAPOTE DEAD," I read. I was stunned. Truman's health had been miserable for the past ten years. But I had never expected this.

I was in Beaufort, a historic town on the coast of South Carolina, alone in my house with my doberman pinscher, Josh, and my rottweiler, Bella. A few years earlier, my husband had purchased an eighteenth-century house in the historic section of the town. We had started renovations. The house was then only a shell with unpainted walls and an unfinished kitchen and bathrooms. That afternoon I had driven the sixty miles from our other house in the small crossroads town of Branchville to Beaufort to supervise the workers who were scheduled to install an underpinning for our double fireplace the next day.

I sat there in shock for several minutes, watching the television screen but not really seeing anything. My dog Bella came over and nuzzled my side. I put my arms around her and felt myself slowly growing numb. Nothing in the room seemed real any more. This famous person known to the world as Truman Capote was dead. But I was not grieving for the famous literary celebrity, that pint-sized man with the voice that was the delight of dozens of mimics.

Rather my thoughts were of a small boy of six or seven who had been brought up in the land of sugar tits and collard greens. He had been my nephew. And I had helped raise him in my cousin Jenny's house in Monroeville, Alabama, so many years ago. No, I could not relate to that puffy-faced man whose face was flushed with defeat that I saw on the television screen. Rather, in my mind's eye, I saw another person, little Truman Persons (he changed his name to Capote after his mother married Joe Capote, who was Cuban, in late 1933) with his jaunty walk, who strode confidently past the Lady Bankshea rosebush in our backyard toward the treehouse, carrying a monstrous Webster's dictionary under one arm. Nelle Harper Lee, his friend and constant companion, was usually at his side, carrying a fruit jar filled with glass marbles that sparkled with more colors than a dozen rainbows. In my mind's eye I watched the two of them climb the trunk of the tree and disappear into their tree house, where none of us adults were ever allowed to enter.

I was grieving for Truman Persons, the son of my sister Lillie Mae Persons, the little boy who could work his way out of any sticky situation as easily as an earthworm can burrow out of the mud after a summer rain shower. This was my Truman, not the rather sad and pathetic man who had mysteriously succumbed during an afternoon nap while visiting the home of Joanne Carson in the Bel-Air section of Los Angeles.

Early the next morning two policemen came to my front door.

"Mrs. Rudisill, we have some news for you," one of them called through the door. "May we come in?"

"No," I replied. "I have two dogs inside. Tell me

through the door. What is it you want?"

"We still think we should be with you when we break the news."

"Officer," I said, "is the news about my nephew Truman Capote?"

"Yes," they responded.

"Thank you for coming," I said. "But I have already heard about his death on television. It was kind of you officers to come. I appreciate it very much."

"Mrs. Rudisill, before we leave, is there anything we can get you, or drive you anywhere?"

"No," I said, "there is nothing you can do."

Later that same morning I called Joanne Carson in California to hear from her just how Truman had died. After she answered her telephone, there was a long minute of strained silence. She and Truman had been the closest of friends for over twenty years.

"Joanne, how did Truman die?" I asked.

Joanne took a deep breath and then told me the story. "Truman had gone to his room to take a nap. He had been complaining of exhaustion earlier in the day. He had asked me to wake him in time for a late afternoon swim. When I went into his room, I found him in a strange state, sort of just fading away. I said, 'Truman, let me call a doctor or take you to a hospital.' 'No,' he insisted softly, grabbing my arm with a bulldog grip. 'If you care for me at all, just let me go.'"

"But why would you let him make a decision like that?" I demanded. "What if he could have been saved by prompt medical treatment?"

At that point I wished I had bit my tongue. Joanne had been one of Truman's oldest and most devoted friends. Had she been able to do anything to save his life, I knew that she would have done it.

Joanne began to weep softly into the telephone.

"Joanne, did Truman leave any kind of manuscript at your house?"

"Yes," she said. "Well, not a manuscript, just some lines he had scrawled on a page of his yellow legal pad. I think they have something to do with *Answered Prayers*."

"Joanne, could you please find that sheet of paper and read me Truman's last words? This is very important."

"Yes, of course," Joanne said and then set down the telephone. She returned after several minutes. "I have it here now. This is what Truman wrote." And then she starting reading in a voice that was surprisingly steady after what she had experienced in the previous twenty-four hours.

"There were flowers everywhere, masses of winter lilac, primrose, and lavender-edged roses. Beautifully bound books lined all the walls in the living room."

Then she stopped.

"Is that all?" I asked.

"Yes, just that fragment. I thought it must have something to do with *Answered Prayers*."

"No, Joanne, just a few weeks ago Truman told me that he was done with *Answered Prayers*. He said it had caused him too much grief and he would never go back to it. I feel sure that this is the beginning of a book he wanted to write about his Southern childhood growing up in Monroeville, Alabama. That passage you just read is a description of his cousin Jenny's house and yard where he spent the first seven years of his life."

My thoughts drifted back almost two months to Truman's call. We had been estranged for far too many years, in one of those silly quarrels that Southern families can sometimes get locked into for years on end. He had been thinking about his child-hood in Monroeville, which had provided him with the experiences he had drawn upon for his first novel and some of his most famous short stories.

And so he had called me late one night in Branchville. We had talked for several hours as if words were the glue that could mend the broken pieces of time and make it whole again. And with the talking, we had also mixed in some laughing and even a little crying.

At this time Truman confided that he had not written anything more on *Answered Prayers*. For the past decade he had pretended to the world and his publisher that he was on top of his situation and that at any time he would complete his book. He had laughed as he told me that every time Joe Fox, his editor at Random House, called him about the project, he would swear that he would have more material the following week. He would then pat a long yellow pad of paper and tell Joe that he had been working on *Answered Prayers* just that day and the manuscript was right next to him as he talked now. Then Truman had laughed again and admitted to me that he had not written another word on that project in years.

Soon people would be searching Truman's house in New York for the rest of *Answered Prayers*. But didn't Joe Fox and the others at Random House understand their famous writer any better than that?

Truman had then told me that he had put that failure behind him and was ready to strike out now in a new direction. He was clearly optimistic that a return to his Southern roots would resurrect his literary reputation.

"I want to write about my own life, about what it meant to be a child in the South back in the 1920s," he told me. He had just read Eudora Welty's memoir, *One Writer's Beginnings*, and it had set him to thinking about his own life. "About Jenny and Sook and Bud and the life we all lived together in that big house," he reflected. "About riding on those big steamboats where my father worked. About tap-dancing while Satchmo and his band played. About all that time."

I snapped back to the present time. I had gotten too far away; I had called Joanne particularly to get the facts of his death. I was still in a state of disbelief.

"I am happy that you and Truman finally mended your differences," Joanne said. "He loved you very much. He was so glad to find out the truth about those abusive telegrams your husband sent him, signing your name."

Before his death Truman had specified to Joanne that I was to handle all the details of his funeral and cremation. Not Jack Dunphy, his lover for thirty-six years. Not Joanne Carson. But me, his aunt. The reason, I think, was that he trusted me to honor his wishes for his final arrangements. My sister, Mary Ida Carter, showed up at Joanne's house two days later, but she couldn't give the authorization for the disposal of Truman's body. And so I sent a telegram to the Westwood Village Park Mortuary, giving them permission to collect the body from the authorities and cremate it, according to my nephew's final wishes.

After I had gotten over the original shock, I was happy that Truman had died at the house of Joanne Carson, one of his closest and dearest friends. He would have celebrated his sixtieth birthday the next month, and Joanne had been planning a black-tie dinner bash to mark the occasion. "He was in terrific spirits Friday night," she told me. "We went swimming and then made plans for his birthday."

The two had met in 1962 when Truman was busy

at work on *In Cold Blood*. She had recently married Johnny Carson, who was then the host of an afternoon television show called *Who Do You Trust?* Soon afterward, he was chosen as the host of the *Tonight Show*. This sudden escalation in fame and fortune thrust Joanne into a very different lifestyle from the one she was used to. She found herself married to one of the most popular men on television and living in a suite at the United Nations Plaza with a limousine on call and celebrities from all walks of life as her social companions. The change in status triggered a host of anxieties.

That was when she met Truman, who was a neighbor at the United Nations Plaza. I think he sympathized with her because of some similarities in their childhoods. Both had been shuttled back and forth among relatives. He took her under his wing, tutoring her in the ways of the rich and famous. He even went so far as to help her select her wardrobe and tell her what outfit she should wear on a particular occasion. She adored her new friend and allowed him to exert considerable control over her life, telling me much later that Johnny was of no help in these matters to her at this time.

After Joanne broke up with Johnny, Truman persuaded her to move back to California where she had been born. She bought a house near UCLA and started her own television talk show, which enjoyed a modest success locally for a time and then was canceled. She had contacted many of the people who had appeared as guests on her husband's show, but few agreed to appear on her show. Truman tried desperately to get her into his so-called "Group A" inner circle, but he never succeeded. He was quite fond of her and so much wanted her to do well. And I think she, in turn, loved him to the point of worship. She always kept a guest room in her house for him, and he often stayed with her when he visited Los Angeles.

Joanne's friendship with Truman lasted twenty-two years and was always filled with whimsy and little games. One evening when he was staying in her guest room, he announced to her, "My precious, I have a treat for you. Tomorrow we go to Paris. Is your passport handy?" Then in the morning after she had awakened, Truman appeared at her bedroom door carrying a tray heaped to overflowing with freshly baked croissants and little jars of jelly from the Crillon Hotel in Paris. "This house was our playpen," she told reporters wistfully after his death.

A bizarre footnote to their friendship happened in October 1988. Joanne hosted a large Halloween party. After the guests had departed, she discovered to her horror that someone had stolen $200,000 worth of jewelry, including a pearl necklace given to her by Johnny and, more importantly, all of her Truman mementos, including a small urn containing a few handfuls of his ashes. Although the bulk of the remains were with Jack Dunphy in Sagaponack, New York, Joanne had kept some of the ashes. As she put it, Truman had wanted to be "bicoastal, even after death."

Then six nights later the ashes reappeared as if by magic. Under cover of darkness, a mysterious car screeched in and out of Joanne's driveway. When Joanne checked later, she discovered Truman's mortal remains resting inside a coil of garden hose on her back steps. She decided to put her small part of Truman in a safer resting place, a vault at the Westwood Memorial Park in Los Angeles. On November 11, 1988, in the company of several cemetery officials, she placed the urn, some mementos, and a letter inside the coffin-size crypt. The letter read, in part: "Tru love, wait for me. I'll be joining you in time, and we'll sail kites against the clear blue sky." She was happy that his remains rested near the ashes of Marilyn Monroe and Natalie Wood, two of his favorite actresses. "Oh, how Truman will like being near Marilyn and Natalie," she had said. "They can dish like there's no tomorrow!"

When I read about this in *People* magazine, I just chuckled. All his life Truman had loved creating chaos and confusion. I could imagine him wherever he was, leaning back and laughing heartily at all the fuss.

Everyone eagerly awaited the coroner's report. I think a lot of people suspected that he might have died from a drug overdose. He certainly had been public about both his alcoholism and his drug abuse, usually with his prescribed medications. "I put them together, like some sort of cocktail," he once admitted during a television interview. He was hospitalized in April 1983 in Montgomery, Alabama, after tests showed he had a toxic level of dilantin and phenobarbitol in his system. At the time his doctors said he had experienced a "bad reaction" to the drugs, which are used to control epileptic seizures. And in

August 1983 he pleaded guilty to a charge of drunken driving on New York's Long Island. (The judge rebuked him for appearing in court wearing Bermuda shorts.)

A month after Truman's death, Ronald Kornblum, Los Angeles County's chief medical examiner/coroner, released his report from a three-hour autopsy he had performed. He concluded that my nephew had died of liver disease complicated by phlebitis and multiple drug intoxication. No alcohol was discovered in his blood. But toxicological tests found barbiturates, Valium, anti-seizure drugs, and painkillers consistent with the numerous prescribed medicines at his bedside. "The toxicity was a contributing factor, but not lethal," the coroner ruled. "If it had not been for the liver problems, the intake of medications would not have been a problem." About the same time I saw a newspaper report that he had left an estate worth just over $600,000.

Truman's death was much easier for me to accept because of our reconciliation eight weeks before after years of estrangement. It had all started over a collection of expensive Baccarat paperweights that I had lent him and he had refused to return. At the time I was living in Charlotte, North Carolina, and working as an antiques dealer, specializing in paperweights. I had a fairly large selection of weights, and in most cases I had not actually paid for them but had bought them on spec, planning to pay for them after selling them to collectors and other dealers.

At that time Truman had his own collection of paperweights, including one, the "White Rose," that had been given to him by Colette, the famous French writer, when he visited her in Paris in 1948. He published an article on the experience in 1970, which he later reprinted in his book *The Dogs Bark: Public People & Private Places.* The two were introduced in her luxurious Old World bedroom, the air of which was saturated with the scent of roses, oranges, and limes. But what really captured his fancy was not the noted personage, who lay propped upon a mountain of lace-edged pillows, with her "slanting, alley-cat eyes rimmed with kohl and lips thin and tense as wire but painted a really brazen hussy scarlet." Rather it was her collection of over one hundred antique paperweights. He called them a "magical exhibition." They dazzled him, capturing his imagination the way few things had. Colette understood his excitement and gave him a Baccarat weight from the nineteenth century, a marvelous, bubble-free, fist-sized piece of crystal with a simple white rose with green leaves sunk dead center.

This piece sent him off on an expensive search for additional antique French paperweights. Whenever he traveled, across the country or abroad, he always took with him two or three of his precious paperweights. Why? Because, as he told me, "When I spread them about, they can make for me the most sinisterly anonymous hotel room seem warm and personal and secure. And because, when it's a quarter to two and sleep hasn't come, a restfulness arises from contemplating a quiet white rose until the rose expands into the whiteness of sleep."

I always knew that Truman was obsessive about his paperweights. But I never realized until his visit to my home in Charlotte in 1973 just how unscrupulous he could be, even toward his favorite aunt. He knew, of course, that I was a dealer of antique paperweights. And so one of the first things he asked was to see my collection. As soon as I brought them out, he was beside himself with excitement. The next thing I knew he had grabbed a pillow from my bed, stripped off its case, and started to fill it up with my weights.

"What in the world are you doing, Truman?" I demanded.

"Darling," he replied, "I am taking these with me because when I am in a hotel I put them on my night table. They are so beautiful and comforting."

"But, Truman, I have those weights to sell. I still owe a great deal of money for them."

"Yes, I know. And I swear I will send them back to you very soon. But, please, let me borrow them, just for a short time."

I was extremely nervous about letting the paper-weights out of my sight. I had just purchased a rather large number of new French Baccarat limited edition weights on an open account and expected to pay for them as I sold them. But against my better judgment I reluctantly let Truman take them away.

Time went by. Truman failed to return my weights, as he had promised. I kept calling and writing him, pleading with him to please send them back. I explained that the bill was due, and I could not pay it. Always his answer was the same: "Darling, I am on my way to Switzerland (or wherever) and promise,

promise, promise you that on my return I will send them all back." He never did. Finally, Baccarat sued me. I was never able to buy wholesale again. Truman's carelessness had destroyed my hope of a career as a dealer of antiques. By then my husband, Jim, who worked in the textile business, was furious because we could not afford to pay for the missing paperweights.

Soon afterward Truman began to grow cool toward me. Gone were the days when he would call from all corners of the world to chat for hours on end on a variety of topics. Then one day I had a call from my sister, Mary Ida. She gave me a full report on a large publicity bash for Truman in Montgomery shortly before. I was stunned because I had not been invited.

"Mary Ida, for heaven's sakes, I never received an invitation," I said.

"Tiny [that was always my family name], I am sure you know why Truman is mad at you," she said.

"No, I haven't any idea," I replied.

"It's all those lewd telegrams you are sending him through Western Union. They are piling up at the desk at United Nations Plaza, and the personnel there are aware of their contents."

For a moment I sat perfectly still. This had all happened so suddenly that I was afraid to speak, fearful that the least whisper, a single breath drawn too deeply, would prevent me from learning more about this dreadful thing of which I had been accused. The silence between us was like a spun thread, fragile and all but breaking.

Finally I said, "I have never sent Truman a telegram in my life."

"Well, he insists that your name was signed to all of them."

"Did you actually see any of them?" I wanted to know.

"Well, yes, Truman showed me several. And, frankly, I do not understand how Western Union let them get through. They were very, very vulgar."

Suddenly, I knew what had happened. My husband Jim had been beside himself over the business concerning the paperweights. He also was a heavy drinker. He had always harbored a good deal of resentment toward Truman over his flamboyant homosexuality, calling him a "slutty fag." I now knew that when he was on the road for business and had

had a little too much to drink, he would send those telegrams, signing my name to them. The telegrams had all come from towns where he had textile accounts. Even after I confronted Jim about this, he continued to send the telegrams behind my back.

In the spring of 1984, I was determined to heal the rift between Truman and myself. I wrote him a long letter, begging him to call me so we could settle our differences. Then two weeks later, much to my surprise and relief, he called me at my home in Branchville. The telephone rang. I picked it up and heard on the other end his familiar greeting, "Hello, darling."

Sure enough, it was Truman's voice. Yet it was not.

"Truman," I said, "are you well?"

"In a way, yes. Doctors at Sloan-Kettering have been treating me for cancer of the rectum. If you call that being well." (I never learned whether or not Truman was telling me the truth about his cancer. From a young age on he had been an outrageous liar, always willing to tell the biggest fib imaginable to score a point or win some sympathy.)

"Why didn't you tell me?"

"Because, darling, I did not know whether or not you really gave a hoot."

"Truman, you know I care very deeply. Remember, I am the one who tried to settle our differences. If I had not loved you so much, I would never have contacted you. I am seventy-three years old and I want to be sure that I make peace with you before I leave this earth."

"Darling, you have a long time to live. Only the good die young, if you get my meaning."

"Truman, why don't you visit me in South Carolina and stay for a while?"

"I will, eventually, but first I must go to California to see Joanne Carson and then to Monroeville. After that, I will visit you."

"Why are you going to Monroeville?" I wanted to know.

"Well, darling, I want to write a book about my childhood in Monroeville, very much along the lines of Eudora Welty's book, *One Writer's Beginnings*. I really want to start, literally speaking, a new life. And it's just like T. S. Eliot said once, 'Home is where we start from.'"

I reflected for a moment.

"Truman, there is no such thing as a 'new life.' Only the turnings and windings and broadening of the old," I said.

"You are wrong, Tiny," he replied. "There is a new life. And I intend to find it and live it. But, please, darling, when I come to South Carolina, do not constantly nag me about my lifestyle and drinking."

"That is an easy promise to make. I long ago realized, Truman, that arguing with you is like lying on a feather bed. I just sink in and get nowhere," I said.

"Come now, darling, don't let 'Miss Nasty' rear her ugly head."

"Well, have you started your book yet?" I asked, changing the subject.

"Yes, yes, darling. I have started writing my book a hundred times. I expect my visit to Monroeville will put me into just the right frame of mind to get into some serious writing," he said.

"What about a title—do you have one yet?" I asked.

"Yes," he replied, "I want to call my book of memories *Where the Lilac Blooms*."

For a moment he was silent. I sensed that his mind was going back to the line of deep purple lilac trees that grew along the fence outside Jenny's house, almost touching our kitchen windows and hiding the pen holding our chickens and turkeys.

Like so many Southern writers of the 1930s and 1940s, who as a group had created the richest, most memorable body of regional literature in the history of American letters, Truman had journeyed north-ward. He had walked down a path that had taken him farther and farther from Monroeville. As the years had passed, his links with his Southern past had grown weaker and weaker. As I look back on those later years, I sense that Truman had a need to cut himself off deliberately from the people and places that gave his childhood meaning and substance to much of his early fiction. When I had complained, he had simply shrugged his shoulders and said, "Darling, why should I deny myself all the richnesses of life which have now opened for me? Wouldn't that be a silly foolishness?"

Truman's disillusionment with his life in the North, unlike that of his literary compatriots, had taken decades to materialize. In the final year of his life, New York City began to seem merely ugly and big. And a part of him yearned for the limitations of the provincial life back home. He never expressed a wish to return physically to live in the South. (I'm certain he would have been miserable, had he tried.) But as an author he had decided in those final months of his life to return to the community of his origin.

New York City and Europe had provided him with the larger half of his life. But the South finally reasserted itself and claimed him once again. I think at the end of his life he must have felt a kinship with the other great literary men and women of the South—William Faulkner, Robert Penn Warren, Thomas Wolfe, Eudora Welty, Katherine Ann Porter, and Ellen Glasgow, to name just a few—who also came from small Southern towns very much like Monroeville, Alabama, where Truman had spent his formative years as a boy. It was from these roots that he had become alienated after his move to New York City. And it was these same cultural roots that drew him back shortly before his death.

"After I have written this next book, I will be content," Truman continued. "The pattern of my life will then be complete."

Our last conversation had lasted almost the entire

night, from 1:00 A.M. until 4:30 A.M. Just before we finally hung up, Truman promised once again to come and visit me in Branchville after his trip to the West.

The next week I bought a copy of Eudora Welty's *One Writer's Beginnings*, eager to read what Truman had called his "beacon in the night, shining the way to a new direction." I was particularly moved by a passage near the very end where she reflected:

> It is our inward journey that leads us through time—forward or back, seldom in a straight line, most often spiraling. Each of us is moving, changing, with respect to others. As we discover, we remember; remembering, we discover; and most intensely do we experience this when our separate journeys converge.

Biography has many cunningly contrived corridors. If we follow this one of literary triumph followed by defeat, we shall see that at the end of his journey Truman's life had come full circle, back to his Southern roots.

The Southern Haunting of
Truman Capote

1

Monroeville, Alabama: Jenny's House

Monroeville, Alabama, where Truman spent his first seven years, is a crossroads town in the Deep South, midway between Montgomery and Mobile. Seventy years ago it was pretty much the same as a hundred other such towns in the South. The architecture of its business section was undistinguished, all the buildings either ugly brick or sunbleached wood with their awnings, once garishly striped, now weather-beaten and torn.

A courthouse with a pyramid-shaped roof and clock tower dominated the center of the square. Chiseled into plain white marble above the entrance were the words MONROE COUNTY COURTHOUSE. (The interior was used in the filming of *To Kill a Mockingbird*.) The sidewalks around the square were paved, but the streets were Alabama clay, which turned into a red mushy mire during the winter rains and restless dust during the summer droughts.

Throughout the warmer months old men congregated on benches on the courthouse grass playing checkers, chewing tobacco, whittling sticks, or simply passing time, their liver-spotted hands crooked on their hickory sticks. It was the sort of place the local undertaker looked at with confidence, knowing that he was never going to starve as long as there was that much work coming his way eventually.

On the one side of the square was Dr. Fripp's general store, a most heavenly place for children. Here one could find candy, toys, crêpe paper, horse collars, and party favors, in addition to kitchen appliances, tools, and other miscellaneous merchandise. Salt mackerel filled wooden barrels. Bins of coffee and pickles in sour-smelling vinegar with flies floating on top surrounded the counter. The old store had never been painted and had aged to a silver gray. The ceiling was so black above the cross rafters where the horse collars hung that the abundance of spiders was no mystery. One wall of Dr. Fripp's store was covered with tin signs advertising chewing tobacco, chicken feed, soft drinks, and Carter's Little Liver Pills.

On the other side of the square was the town drugstore. An old metal sign flapped in the breeze out front, its gilt background long since peeled away; the name, MONROE DRUGS, had almost faded away completely. The interior was filled with ancient wire-legged tables surrounded by rickety chairs and a marvelous white-marble counter that boasted a row of high stools in front and a streaked mirror behind. There you went to get your prescription filled by Mr. Yarborough, the druggist, provided you did not come between noon and one o'clock because that was lunchtime. Kids on their way home from school, toting shoulder bags, always stopped by the drugstore to order a lemon Coke, a cherry pop, or a banana split.

Monroeville's heart was the square, with the rest of our town radiating beyond. Many of the houses were large and encrusted with the opulent gingerbread ornamentation that had been the popular architectural style for so many years. The streets were lined with great oaks, heavy with curtains of matted moss that swung softly in the evening breezes. There were three churches—the Baptist, the Methodist, and the Mount Zion, the last for the Negroes. (Our family belonged to the Baptist.)

This was an earlier America of ladies' sewing circles and garden clubs, church socials, a solitary picture show that exhibited movies only on Friday and Saturday (silent, of course, with a piano accompaniment), of weddings with old shoes and white ribbons and county fairs with blue ribbons for the best cakes and pies. As in so many Southern towns in the early part of this century, people in Monroeville were born, lived, and died without ever once thinking seriously about moving away. The descendants of the original families, who had settled the wilderness when Indians roamed the forests, farmed their lands, ran their businesses, and married into other families just as old, sometimes too close to the bloodlines.

Truman's happiest years as a youth were spent in this town. Jenny, Callie, Sook, and Bud Faulk were the distant cousins with whom he shared his childhood. None had ever taken a mate. They all lived together under Jenny's firm hand in a huge, rambling white frame house, very near the square, that was cool and delightful in summer but too drafty and cold in the winter. It was the kind of home that gathers memories like dust, a place filled with laughter and joy, pain and heartbreak.

To us children (for Jenny's house had been my home too, and the home of Truman's mother, Lillie Mae), the entrance hall alone appeared as large as the average small house. The ceilings seemed to reach to the beyond. About halfway down the hall, Jenny had built bookcases on either side, flanked by two round pillars that rose with great majesty to the ceiling. Whenever I entered the house, those towering pillars always caught my eyes, pulling them upward to the ornate scrollwork on top.

The dining room represented Jenny and her life of careful acquisition. The furniture, even the silver and china, had been the same for at least thirty years. Along one wall a serpentine-front china cabinet overflowed with Dresden, Meissen, and sparkling pieces of cut glass. Jenny would tap a piece of glass with her fingernail, making a bell-like sound, or pick up a piece of Meissen and say, "This belonged to Aunt Fronie." Her pride was a Lunnuier dining-room table with Anthony Quervelle sideboard. The imposing set was large and heavy in appearance. It suited

Jenny perfectly. She loved her antiques, and yet she did not regard them as museum pieces. Never did she reprimand a child for touching any of her prizes. I recall one occasion when she allowed the young Truman to shake the prisms on the enormous basket chandelier to set them dancing and tinkling.

A wide verandah went around the front of the house and disappeared in the back. The backyard was a both a delight and a frustration. Trellis upon trellis held twisted, tortured wisteria vines, which hung like an ominous blue curtain, blotting out our view of the town. The yard was filled to overflowing with japonicas, azaleas, and walls of blue hydrangeas. Somehow each spring the King Alfred daffodils managed to rear their heads and bloom. There was no order or rhythm to the garden.

Surrounding this landscaper's nightmare was a tall fence made of animal bones. Jenny had ordered them hauled to Monroeville from an animal graveyard in Clairborne, Alabama, and then supervised the selection and laying of each bone as the fence slowly took shape. "No," she would say firmly, "the backbone can't be next to the foot bone; that isn't right. You have to fit the backbone to the hipbone." And so the gruesome fence was finally completed after many months of hawk-eyed supervision. I remember being told how one worker had bumped his wheelbarrow into the fence, causing an avalanche of bones to come crashing down, at which point Jenny had given him such a tongue-lashing that he took off like a scared jackrabbit and never returned. To Jenny, the fence was a triumphant achievement, a monumental tribute to things dead, living, and yet to come. The house has since burned down (in 1952, to be rebuilt on the same foundations), but Jenny's bone fence still stands, grimly defying fire and the elements.

Jenny was a beautiful woman, even in her fifties. She had frosty blue eyes, hair the color of red oak leaves in autumn, and skin like a china doll, translucent in its dazzling whiteness. Her hands were strong and squarish with faint freckles, like a pear ready to be picked. She was born as stylish as a tomcat with white paws and waistcoat. She was on the short side, but her sharp tongue gave her added stature.

Jenny's dry goods store on the town square was the dream of any young girl. As you came through the front door, there was a huge showcase that covered about twelve feet of wall and was filled with perfumes and expensive cosmetics. Next there was a long counter with yard measures cut into the wood. Behind the counter were shelves holding stacks and stacks of calicoes, solid-colored percales, and bolts of cloth of every description—stripes, dots, and figures. On the floor were bins that overflowed with lace, embroidery, rickrack braid in bright, bold colors, and soutache braid in gold, silver, and brilliant red. Against the opposite wall were cases filled with Vanity Fair silk undergarments, and silk stockings hung from the wall behind. Jenny's pride was her front picture window that she had had shipped in from New Orleans. The top border of the window was actually cut glass, large diamond-shaped fans that appeared to explode in the sunlight.

About the same time Jenny built her store, she also built the large, rambling frame house that would be her home—and Truman's—for so many years. Samantha, Callie, Sook, and Bud all settled with her in Monroeville. Jenny thus made her home into a refuge for her mother, two sisters, and brother. Her own personal pleasures always came second to her responsibilities to her family and business. She never married, but she did have her lovers, although we never knew for certain about them. In the front yard hidden beneath the rosebushes was a small tombstone that read simply, "ONE DAY OLD." Jenny would never answer our questions about it, but Callie, her sister, whispered—perhaps with more spite than truth—that it was the grave of a stillborn illegitimate child Jenny had had by a lover in St. Louis, where she went often on buying trips.

Corrie, our Negro house servant, summed it up best of all: "Miz Jenny is what I calls a high-vitality female."

Callie, Jenny's younger sister, had been a schoolteacher until Jenny forced her to quit to help out in the store. Like a boa constrictor crushing its prey, the older sister completely dominated the younger. Even though she had been baptized Caroline Elizabeth, she was known throughout her life as Callie, a name she detested, insisting it sounded like the name of a Negro maid. This was Jenny's name for her and it stuck. Whatever name Jenny used, the rest of the family and town took up. So poor Callie was denied even the dignity of her own name.

Callie was a severe woman with gray eyes as hard as rifle balls. She had a precise, thin upper lip and round chin that always quivered violently just before the tears came in the many confrontations with her sister. Her hair was coal black, and she wore it bobbed all her life. She had tiny feet that she always pampered in later years with shoes of the softest leather. Her waist was the envy of many a younger woman. Bud would often tell her, "Not a girl in the whole town has a waist like yours, Caroline. Why, a man could get his two hands around it with plenty of room to spare!" (Bud, by the way, was the only one to defy Jenny on the matter of Callie's name and call her Caroline.)

Nancy, or Sook, as she was known to the family, was Jenny's older sister and Truman's favorite. She exerted a profound influence, not always constructive, on the young boy.

Sook was the kind of person who loved all living things. All stray animals, stray children, anything in need, became a part of her. And in 1924 when baby Truman was brought to Jenny's home in Monroeville, Sook cared for him as though he were a gift from heaven. He filled a void for her and gave her life meaning.

Sook was all innocence, unable to adapt to the

demands of the world at large. She possessed a child-like perception of life that she never lost. She was the most fragile, dependent, and vulnerable of the family group. Jenny's house really *was* her refuge in a more immediate way than it was for the others.

John Byron, or Bud as everyone called him, was the older brother. He was a good-natured, kind man but weak and unable to assert himself in the family, a failure by the traditional definitions of the word. His pride was the six hundred acres he had inherited from his father's plantation. He never worked a day in his life, and he never did anything with his land except let Sylvester, an ancient black man, sharecrop part of the farm to grow a little cotton.

In all important matters, especially those involving business, Jenny rigidly excluded Bud, never even asking his advice. She allowed her brother only one responsibility in her house. He was to act as host and master of the house, but only at the dining-room table. There he sat at the head and carved the roasts and fowls that came in from the kitchen. Bud said the blessing, served the plates, and kept a sharp eye on our behavior.

Our dining-room table at Jenny's sat ten comfortably. Whatever children there were sat at smaller tables placed to one side, each of which was set with linen, silver, and food exactly like the big table. It has always been a Southern custom to invite over for Sunday dinner those who were new in town, or had a sickness in the family, or had just had a death. So we never knew who might be there.

Our Sunday dinners never varied. We had steak with brown gravy, fresh yellow corn on the cob with lots of melted butter, and fresh yellow squash with onions. There were platters of tomatoes when in season, cucumbers, hot peppers, bell peppers, and a big bowl of boiled okra. When we were young, it was fun to hold our heads back and let the moist, slimy Okra slide down out throats. All Southern children got whacked for doing this disgusting thing at the dinner table, and we Faulk kids (and later Truman) were certainly no exception. Little Bit would bring in big plates of high buttermilk biscuits and steaming "lace corn pone." For dessert we had freshly baked blackberry cobbler buried beneath mounds of whipped cream, or pound cake with a crusty top, or the best pecan pie in the state (or so Bud used to tell Little Bit).

And sometimes ice cream. Often during the summer months we would gather in the backyard and make fresh ice cream. Peach, strawberry, and blackberry were our favorite flavors. We would fill the hand-operated freezer with freshly sliced fruit, thick cream, sugar, custard, and whatever and then pack in the ice. The children would have the honor of pouring the rock salt around the edge and slowly turning the handle, being careful not to let the salt get on top. Finally, after what seemed like hours, the ice cream would harden and be ready to serve.

There were two other people in our household in 1924 when the baby Truman came to live with us: Little Bit, our black cook, and Corrie, the black house servant. Both had lived on the premises for as long as I could remember and had become by then an integral part of the family circle.

Lillie Mae and I ended up at Jenny's house in 1919 after the deaths of our parents, Popper from a kick to his head by his favorite stallion and Mother from a cerebral hemorrhage three years later. Lillie Mae was fourteen at the time; I was seven.

The clashes between Jenny and Lillie Mae started at an early date and lasted a lifetime. My sister was a problem child even then—headstrong, disobedient, independent, and boy crazy. She tried to act and dress as though she were six years older. In fact, Lillie Mae was a flapper even before flappers became popular. She loved to go into Jenny's room and raid her jewelry box. She would pull out ropes of pearls and hang them around her neck and put gold bracelets on each arm. Then she would unbutton her dress in front and dab perfume between her breasts and under her arms. Thus decked out, she would sashay boldly out the front door on her way to school. Jenny would grab her by her skirt and drag her back inside the house, stripping off the jewelry.

"Get back in here this minute, young lady!" Jenny would holler at Lillie Mae. "By all that is holy, you won't leave my house looking like some trash from Rooktown. If I see you again in public with paint on your lips and stinking from all that perfume, you will live to regret it. Do you understand me, Lillie Mae?"

"You're not my mother, Jenny Faulk. You can't boss me like that. I ain't your slave. Don't tell me what to do. I'm grown up," Lillie Mae would scream back, tears welling up in her eyes.

"I may not be your mother, girl, but I am your

guardian," Jenny would insist. "I put food in your stomach, clothes on your body, and a roof over your head. So you show me some respect."

"God, I hate you, Jenny Faulk," Lillie Mae would cry, going to her room and slamming the door so hard that it almost jumped off its hinges.

Lillie Mae continued to be a problem for Jenny. She was disobedient, surly, and ungrateful. At sixteen, she was a spoiled child in the body of a woman. She plucked her eyebrows, rouged the dimples on her knees, and walked with a twitch in her buttocks that mesmerized the boys in her school. Often she wore an ankle chain—a "slave bracelet," she called it—that an older boy had given her.

Lillie Mae became more desperate with the passing of each day. She had to get out of Monroeville and to New Orleans, no matter what. Life in Jenny's home was too confining. She longed for the excitement of the big city—for a world of money and class, of fast men, fast cars, and expensive restaurants.

Suddenly, in the early part of the summer of 1923, Lillie Mae's ticket to that fantasy world appeared in Monroeville, riding in a fancy chauffeur-driven black Packard and sporting one of the most prominent names in the state of Alabama. He was Archulus Persons—Arch for short. True, he was not much to look at—about as far from movie-star good looks as you could get. But his family name meant a great deal. His father had been a prominent chemistry professor at the University of Alabama in Tuscaloosa and had once been called to Washington to confer with President Theodore Roosevelt on some matter. His grandfather had been a governor of Alabama. His mother was a Knox, from one of the wealthiest families in the entire state and highly influential in government and business circles.

Lillie Mae and Arch had seen each other at a distance, but as yet there had been no formal introduction. But both were interested in the other—Arch in Lillie Mae for her good looks, and Lillie Mae in Arch for the money and social prestige that his name represented.

"You can't miss that Arch Persons in Troy because he is always riding around high and mighty in the backseat of his chauffeur-driven black Packard," Lillie Mae told me. (Later she learned that Arch's car, with its uniformed black chauffeur, belonged to his grandmother, Mrs. Knox.) "And he always wears the most god-awful cream-colored panama hat, which he tilts at a crazy angle on the back of his head. But it does make him look a bit like a rake. And he loves to wear candy-cane-striped silk shirts with white linen suits that have 'MONEY' written all over them."

The two finally met. After a whirlwind courtship, Lillie Mae and Archie married on August 12, 1923, in a grand wedding paid for by Jenny. She gave a huge dinner for the entire wedding party, and there were luncheons and teas all over town. Lillie Mae was the bride but Jenny, as usual, was the queen of the show. She personally greeted all the guests. She had just turned fifty, but you could never have guessed her age from the way she looked that day. On her fingers she had diamond rings that flashed in the sunlight. Around her neck hung a gold chain studded with rubies and diamonds. Jenny had reached that age when she did not have to depend on her sexuality to achieve her objectives. Yet she never for a moment neglected her femininity. Men smiled at her cordially. They respected and liked her as a business figure, but they also found her pleasing as a woman.

After the honeymoon, Arch and Lillie Mae settled in New Orleans. For a while she lived out her dream.

They lived in one of the nicest residential hotels. Arch pampered her with moonlight boat rides on the Mississippi River, dinners at top-name restaurants, and dancing in nightclubs until the sun came up.

In time Lillie Mae became homesick for Monroeville, especially the big Sunday dinners at Jenny's house. She and Arch would arrive on Saturday evening, stay for Sunday dinner, and then head back to New Orleans about 3:00 P.M. Lillie Mae would always tell Jenny, "I'm hungry for some good old-fashioned Southern home-cooking."

Within a few months, Lillie Mae found herself pregnant. She looked ahead to the birth with dread. Emotionally, she was still a child, quite incapable of seeing beyond her own selfish needs. Her imagination worked overtime exaggerating the pain of the birth itself. She dreaded the sleepless nights and the damage to her breasts that might come with feeding her infant. She intensely disliked the interruption in her life that motherhood involved. All these fears caused Lillie Mae to look upon Truman, when he finally did arrive, as a terrible nuisance and an unacceptable obstacle that threatened her carefully constructed plans for moving into the Social Register.

Lillie Mae had neither the strength nor the courage to cope with the ordeal of motherhood. She once told me that she blamed Arch for her pregnancy and resented him for it. Lillie Mae felt that he had betrayed her and his love for her. Thus, she turned her pregnancy into resentment against Arch rather than letting it become the joy it should have been. She never forgave Arch or Truman. After his birth Lillie Mae continued in her own life with as few interruptions as possible. She was never able to devote herself to the needs of her child or to identify herself with his interests as he grew older.

Truman was born on September 30, 1924. Lillie Mae's anxieties made it a difficult birth. As soon as she could check out of the hospital, she took her baby straight to Monroeville. On the day that Lillie Mae placed Truman in her arms, Jenny looked as though she might have owned every stick and stone in the state of Alabama and been willing to chuck them all for him. I am certain Jenny had known long before then that the responsibility for raising the child would fall on her shoulders, but she never flinched.

When Truman arrived in Jenny's home in 1924,

he was the fourth generation of Faulks to find refuge under her roof. There he was to spend the first seven years of his life and have experiences that would later inspire some of his finest writing.

2
A Christmas Memory

Sook was Truman's favorite of all of us who lived under the roof of her sister Jenny's big house. She was a constant companion to her young cousin during those years he spent in Monroeville. After Lillie Mae and Arch literally abandoned their infant son with us, it was Sook, more than any other person, who had the responsibility for his daily care. The two shared many adventures in that time. Much later, after Sook died in January of 1946 and after Truman had become famous, he put her at the center of three of his most popular pieces—*The Grass Harp, The Thanksgiving Visitor,* and *A Christmas Memory.* Sook's influence on Truman was profound.

Sook was one of those obscure spinsters who spend their entire lives in limbos created especially for them on the outer fringes of large families. It was as if, years before at her father's death, the family had simply put her in a corner and forgotten about her, the way you do with a floor lamp or a piece of bric-a-brac. She had no social life at all and no clearly defined sphere of responsibility in the household. Her sisters and brother regarded her as a sort of child who had grown older but never up.

Sook was like a little shadow in the mainstream of our lives, but she taught us many good things. From her we learned to love and respect nature, to care for helpless and friendless creatures, and to see beauty in things that otherwise went unnoticed.

Sook was a small woman, under five feet tall and weighing less than a hundred pounds, but as bouncy as a coiled steel wire. Many years before she had had all her teeth pulled, but Jenny could never persuade her to keep the "store-bought" dentures in her mouth for long. As a result, her jaws had shrunk, giving her a somewhat ghoulish appearance. For as long as I can remember, Sook wore her white hair cropped close to her head. She was a quiet, gentle woman, always in the background, never demanding and rarely receiving. She was the winsome but homely moss rose who wandered at will, taking care to keep out from underfoot of her sisters and brother.

Sook almost always dressed in the same manner. Her dress was a shapely gingham, preferably blue with small checks, and a white apron with two huge pockets in front which she tied behind in a big bow. She never outwardly showed any affection for any of us, except for Truman, whom she adored. But in her own way she was kind to all of us.

We never thought twice about Sook's little idiosyncrasies, though she was highly eccentric. We simply accepted them as normal for her. For instance, Sook was always suspicious of the night air. As a result, she rarely left the house after dusk. Outside, she insisted, lurked the clammy miasma, the deadly swamp fever, and the eternal dampness that could kill a body. For protection she always kept her bedroom windows tightly sealed, no matter how hot and sticky the summer nights might become.

At the beginning of each day Sook would hold her Bible tightly in her hands against her breasts and ask God to send her a message to guide her through that particular day. If the sun was shining, she would be reluctant to stay inside. Instead she would prefer to poke her way through the tangle of flowers and bushes in our backyard, muttering to herself, "Where is that old cantankerous brood hen, Mizzie? Gone off to the woods somewhere and hidden, that's where! Never mind. When she gets hungry, she'll be back!"

Sook had a talent for mixing colors and sketching. I always thought that if she had been encouraged and perhaps had received some formal training, she might have developed into an artist. Her favorite subjects were butterflies, songbirds, and blooming plants. During the long winter evenings Sook would sit and cut pictures from the stack of magazines the household set aside for her. Some of the pictures she used to decorate the kites she loved to make. Others she would carefully trim, then she painted on their backs a thin solution of flour and water and pasted them on the sides of wastebaskets. Some evenings she and Truman would sort through the stacks of pictures she had saved, discussing how each could be best used. Many of them, Sook insisted, were simply too beautiful to cut up. Those were just to keep and look at often.

Over the years Sook had carefully ordered her

life around her "hankerings," her name for those activities that completely preoccupied her attention and time at certain months of the year. She posted a list of them on the kitchen wall and followed it faithfully. Whenever we wanted to know what Sook was doing, we could go to that list and read the activity for the month, which never varied from year to year:

> *January and February: cut out pictures.*
> *March: plant bulbs for the spring flowers.*
> *April: make soft soap.*
> *May: collect roots and herbs.*
> *June: make dropsy medicine.*
> *July: bake cakes and give them away.*
> *August and September: canning and preserving.*
> *October: prepare fruitcakes.*
> *November: fix cheese straws for Thanksgiving.*
> *December: prepare Christmas decorations and gifts.*

Sook's bedroom was located just off the kitchen. This was perfect, as her biggest love was cooking and preserving. She filled our pantry to capacity with all sorts of jellies and preserves; she carefully arranged everything according to its color. Sook made our pantry into her own personal art gallery. She had a clear conception of just what colors ought to sit next to each other on the shelves. Her own favorites were the clear, red-amber mayhaw jellies that, she thought, looked best next to the jars of yellow cling peaches, brandied in applejack. The purplish red strawberries, the pear preserves, the pale pink cherries, the dark brown "Turkey" figs—everything found its place on our pantry shelves according to Sook's own color index system, the logic of which the rest of us understood only imperfectly.

Our kitchen was immense, probably the largest room in the house. The cast-iron wood-burning stove belonged to Sook and Little Bit, our black cook. Jenny had ordered it in St. Louis. The big black cook stove was like an altar with its lofty turreted range trimmed with nickel and the name "Old Buckeye" cast on the front of the big oven door. There were four cooking eyes, a warmer for biscuits and bread, a hot-water tank on one side, and a huge baking oven below. It was trimmed in gleaming solid brass. Sook kept a pot of coffee boiling on the stove, day and night. The aroma of the coffee boiling mingled with the smells of the wood smoke and dishes cooking. She took hers with lots of sugar.

We all gathered around to help Corrie, our black housekeeper, black the stove once a week. She would bring out a tin of polish and a brush. The cooler the stove, the easier the polish went on. We used crumpled newspapers to polish the surface and make it shine like a mirror.

How we loved that old stove. There was always something cooking on one of its eyes and cornbread or biscuits in the warming compartment on the top.

❧ ❧ ❧

Born in 1871, six years after the Civil War ended, Sook had learned the value of creating something from nothing. Knowledge about herbs and spices gleaned from the Creek Indians living on the bank of the Alabama River at Claiborne was a mainstay of Sook's experience and was always reflected in her cooking.

Little Bit, the cook, was very disturbed over Sook's takeover of her pantry, but she was even more upset over her pots of plants and herbs. They were a sight to see, the tall, bushy ones in the back, the smaller ones next, and in the front row the dainty, frilly ones. Sook made her part of the kitchen into a real jungle and even allowed two chameleons to roam freely among them. Regardless of Little Bit's scorn, the two lizards lived happily there, licking drops of water off the foliage with their flicking pink tongues. If you looked carefully, you could see each chameleon curled around the base of its favorite pot, sound asleep, wearing the brown color that indicates a relaxed lizard.

† † †

One of my favorite memories of Sook is that of her sitting before an early October open fire with her big black cat, Joshua, soaking up the warmth. Sook would, after a while, pick Joshua up and settle him in a limp line across her knee, head-on to the fire. His front paws worked at her knee bones with steady prickles, and we were all satisfied that the world was good.

Sook was a great influence on the young Truman simply because she included him in most of her activities. Whether it was constructing kites, gathering herbs, hunting pecans for the fruitcakes, making dolls out of grass, or tinting sandpaper for the fireplace matchboxes, Sook and Truman were certain to be seen working contentedly together, oblivious to the rest of the world.

We had in our backyard an ancient fig tree that

each year yielded a bountiful supply of fruit. Sook loved figs and ate them by the dozen when they were in season. One afternoon during the summer when Truman was six and I was nineteen, she filled her apron full of quarter-size purplish figs and carried them over to where we sat in the shade of an oak tree. She peeled the skin back from the top of a fig and then popped it, oozing and gummy, into Truman's open mouth.

"Pon my word, Miz Sook," Corrie called from the side window, "let dat chile do somethin' fer hisself. Yore actin' like an ole mother hen a-feedin' her own. De onliest thing is, dat chile ain't yore own a'tall."

Sook ignored Corrie and continued to feed Truman.

"Oh, Sook," he cried in happiness, "they are so-o-o-o good."

"I didn't get as many as I hoped to this morning because we waited until too late in the day," she told him. "The birds have eaten holes in the sides of lots of the figs."

"What about that green snake that lives near the fig tree? Doesn't he eat our figs, too?" Truman wanted to know.

Truman referred to the bright emerald-green snake that had taken up residence in our garden near the fig tree. We saw him often in the fig tree, wound around a limb. Sook always insisted that he was up there to eat his fill of the figs but not to worry as there were enough for all of us. Sook would never let us catch that snake or harm him in any way.

"I don't like that snake eating any of our figs," Truman pouted. "I'm going to catch that creepy thing and stomp him to death. Just you watch, Sook."

Sook suddenly became extremely agitated. "Now, Truman," she said very seriously and with tears in her eyes, "don't you ever harm that snake of ours. He has a right to exist, just like the two of us. The good Lord put him here in this garden for us to enjoy, just the same way He put that fig tree here. So, if you want to keep Sook's love, you show some love for that snake."

✦ ✦ ✦

The dog Queenie also figures prominently in *A Christmas Memory*, as a constant companion to Sook and the young Truman when they were on their adventures. Queenie was a black-and-white-spotted rat terrier who became Truman's inseparable companion for many of those years in Monroeville.

The dog came to us late one night in autumn. A nasty cold rain had fallen most of the evening. Truman was out on the back porch when he suddenly spotted a very wet and very miserable puppy curled up in the ray of light coming through the kitchen window. He carefully wrapped the shivering dog in a blanket and carried him to his bedroom, where he hid him for several days, feeding him scraps he had managed to scavenge from the kitchen. But then Jenny, hearing strange noises, investigated and found the dog. She was not happy. Jenny had no use for pets of any sort around her home, especially dogs. But Truman was adamant. He swore up and down that he would take care of the puppy so that he would never bother anyone. Jenny finally relented.

The strange part was that Queenie was a male dog. One day soon after the puppy was established as the newest member of the household, Bud asked Truman, "What are you going to name your dog?"

"His name is Queenie," Truman replied.

"No, Truman," Bud persisted, "you can't call him Queenie. That's a girl's name. You will have to name him Spot or Rover or something like that."

"The dog's name is Queenie, and that's all there is to it," Truman insisted emphatically. And that settled that.

Queenie continued as an integral part of our household long after Truman left Monroeville. Finally, years later, he was killed, kicked in the head by a neighbor's horse. "I wrapped Queenie in a fine linen sheet and rode him in the buggy to Simpson's pasture where he can be with all his bones," Sook wrote Truman, who was by then far away in New York City.

⁜ ⁜ ⁜

One of Sook and Truman's favorite activities was the annual fall preparation of the fruitcakes. Later Truman wrote about these experiences at some length in *A Christmas Memory*. Sook was a teetotaler herself, but she loved to douse her fruitcakes with good whiskey. Of course, during Prohibition she had to use moonshine corn whiskey. Sook bought hers from Victorio, a rather mean-tempered Indian who lived in a shack on the banks of the Little River about eight miles from Monroeville. He ran a fishing camp and, some people insisted, a whorehouse. We never knew for certain about the latter. He was a huge, gap-toothed man with a sallow complexion. Victorio was ugly, and he was tough. (Truman put him in *A Christmas Memory* as Mr. Haha Jones.)

Victorio claimed to be a full-blooded Apache who had come to the Little River from New Mexico. He told us he was named for the famous Apache guerrilla fighter Victorio, who went on the warpath against the whites in the 1880s and was finally killed in a fight with Mexican troops a few years later.

Victorio's whiskey must have been good because lots of people in the county drank it, but he was his own best customer and stayed drunk most of the time. Sook was an old customer from way back, always buying the whiskey for her fruitcakes from "Chief Victorio," as she insisted upon calling him.

"Chief Victorio, it is not good for you to drink so much of your whiskey," Sook once cautioned him.

"The white man crazy over tobacco, the Indian crazy over whiskey," was his answer.

Victorio's fishing camp was a bad place, all right. Many unpleasant things had happened there— fights, knifings, beatings, and even an occasional shooting. One time Victorio lost his patience with a rowdy customer and knocked him into a roaring fire. Or so the stories insisted. But his camp was always quiet when we were there.

When the rest of us accompanied Sook on one of her whiskey-buying expeditions, it was, we thought, an adventure fraught with terrible dangers. We always approached Victorio's camp with extreme caution, never knowing what awful atrocities might happen while we were there. Sook, on the other hand, never had the slightest hesitation. Victorio showed great tenderness and regard for Sook and her fruitcakes, and he always gave her a friendly welcome.

"Please, Chief Victorio," Sook would say, after they had made small talk for several minutes, "we would like two quarts of your best whiskey."

Each October she would offer to pay him for his whiskey, but Victorio would always refuse. "Very well, Chief Victorio," Sook would promise, "I will bring you two of my fruitcakes." She would, too. The big Indian loved her fruitcakes. He would pull up a wooden crate and a bottle of his moonshine whiskey and eat big chunks of the cake while slugging away at his bottle.

Everybody knew that Victorio had a wife, but none of us had ever seen her. Truman had read somewhere that among the Apaches it was customary to disfigure an erring wife by cutting off her nose. We wondered—did Victorio keep his wife hidden because he had amputated her nose in a fit of drunken jealousy? We never found out.

✠ ✠ ✠

No holiday lays its warm hand on our hearts as Christmas does. Then, as at no other time of year, we turn away from the company of strangers to find the few who are close and dear and understanding. With them we renew the fire and color and rhythm of our lives.

On Christmas morning in the Faulk home the smell of lard and hotcake batter was sweet in the kitchen. We always ate the breakfast hotcakes by the open fire, our only nourishment until Christmas dinner at three in the afternoon.

When Jenny flipped on the light switch in the dining room Christmas afternoon, we entered a place such as we might read about but never imagined we would see. The table, a Chippendale with the banquet end on, seated twelve people comfortably. The tablecloth was softly glowing red satin, laid with delicate damask napkins and fine white china bordered by an inch of pure gold. The chandelier of a hundred shining eyes reflected the gleaming silver and crystal. We had everything from a twenty-five-pound turkey and wild strawberry preserves to Sook's fruitcake and poinsettia cake.

Each year, as I slipped into my chair, my eyes took everything in. I received, as at no other time in my life, a sense of abundance, where nothing was stinted and cost was never considered.

3
The Grass Harp

Sook's love for Truman was almost unnatural in its intensity. In her loneliness she desperately clung to the small boy the way a drowning man clutches his piece of flotsam. Perhaps she sensed in Truman a kindred spirit. They were both forgotten people, Sook by her sisters and brother, Truman by his parents. And both were outsiders—Sook because her childlike innocence kept her apart from the adult world, and Truman because his pretty looks, delicate build, and girlish tenderness offended other people's notions of how a "real boy" ought to look and act.

Truman clung to Sook and Sook to Truman. She much preferred that he play with her than with the other children. Sook thought up endless ways to entertain Truman and fill his days. She pampered him beyond all reason, absorbing him into her own unnatural fantasy world. Much about their relationship was unhealthy.

"Miz Nanny, ain't right for you to take up dat chile's time," Corrie would say. "You let him play with de other chillun. Don't you go keeping him so close all de time."

But Sook refused to listen. If the weather turned bad or the complaints of the household became too bothersome, she and Truman would retreat to the attic. This was a favorite adventure for both of them. There they could be together in their own private world and completely escape the real world below. Our attic was a place of mystery, filled with dust and cobwebs and crammed to the overflowing with old trunks, boxes of oddments, a gilt rocking horse, a tattered dress dummy, a wheelchair, and broken wicker furniture—old worthless things that counted for nothing except to Sook and Truman, for whom they opened up new imaginary worlds. Together they searched through the boxes and barrels to bring forth from hidden places the finery of an earlier life—folded paisley shawls, fancy hand-crocheted doilies, fine linen petticoats with handmade lace and tiny, tiny tucks, even old Valentines that had grown brittle and yellow with age. Sook loved to sort through the collection of old clothes and dress Truman up, putting a bonnet on his head, slipping faded white arm-length gloves on his hands, wrapping a feathered boa around his neck, and fitting his feet into embroidered slippers that had grown stiff with age. "Pshaw, Tru," she would say, "don't you look like an elegant lady ready for the ball!"

※ ※ ※

Truman published his short novel *The Grass Harp* in 1951 and once again set Sook at the center in the character of Dolly Talbo. He opened his story with a note of reminiscence: "When was it that first I heard of the grass harp? Long before the autumn we lived in the china tree; an earlier autumn, then; and, of course, it was Dolly who told me, no one else would have known to call it that, a grass harp."

In Truman's novella the grass harp is a field of Indian grass between River Woods and the hilltop cemetery outside a small Southern town. In autumn the wind turns it into a "harp of voices" that tells the story of all the people buried on the hill, "of all the people who ever lived."

Where the field of Indian grass joins a woods, there is a double-trunked chinaberry tree that holds an ancient tree house, as easy to reach as climbing stairs. The narrator Collin Fenwick, Dolly, and her closest friend Catherine Creek, the black house servant, retreat there when the pressures of the world close in upon them—surely the dream of many a child—and find happiness for a short time.

The Grass Harp was Truman's favorite of all his works, but many critics have found it flawed by an excess of sentimentality. Bob Linscott, his editor then at Random House, never liked it. He was the one who gave it the title. Truman's first title was *Summer's Crossing*, which he later changed to *Music of the Sawgrass*. Bob always thought the story's ending was weak. Truman had gotten his characters up in the treehouse and then didn't know what to do with them, he insisted. Bob asked him to rewrite the ending. But Truman was never able to make enough changes to please Bob and finally gave up trying.

In *The Grass Harp*, the character of Dolly earns a small income by making and selling a dropsy cure she had learned years before from a group of gypsies who had passed through the area. Each year her close friend Catherine and the young narrator help her collect the herbs and make the medicine.

> Dolly hover[ed] over the tub dropping our grain-sack gatherings into the boiling water and stirring, stirring with a sawed-off broomstick the brown-as-tobacco spit brew. She did the mixing of the medicine alone while Catherine and I stood watching like apprentices to a witch. We all helped later with the bottling of it and, because it produced a fume that exploded ordinary corks, my particular job was to roll stoppers of toilet paper. Sales averaged around six bottles a week, at two dollars a bottle. The money, Dolly said, belonged to the three of us, and we spent it as fast as it came in.

This is a pretty accurate description of what was Sook's major project every year, the preparation of her dropsy medicine each June. When her mother, Samantha, lay on her deathbed years before, she had whispered to her daughter a strange message. Sook was to visit an Indian medicine man and shaman near Clairborne who would give her a secret recipe for an

Indian medicine made from herbs and roots that was certain to cure dropsy. (Dropsy is a strange disease that causes water to accumulate in the tissues, so that the person becomes bloated all over.) Samantha evidently thought that if Sook were able to make and sell this medicine, she would have some small measure of financial security.

Sook kept large sacks of strange herbs and roots in our smokehouse. Every May she and Truman scoured the surrounding woods, gathering what she needed for her medicine. What she couldn't find she purchased or bartered from her shaman friend at the Creek reservation outside Clairborne. Sook took great delight in telling us the names of the roots and herbs in her bags, but she never revealed how she used them. Some of them, such as cinchona, jalap, pennyroyal, and agave, were quite exotic, often coming from foreign countries. Sook was terribly proud of her collection.

Our garden would be in full bloom by June. Freshly cut roses would be in most of the rooms, and their scent would permeate the entire house. Then one day we would hear from the back the sounds of a fire being made and water being poured into a large black cast-iron pot—the sounds every June that announced the start of Sook's medicine preparation.

"Jenny," Callie would demand, "why do you let that damn fool sister of ours make that vile-smelling concoction?"

"Be patient, Callie," Jenny would reply. "In another week Sook will be done with her medicine. It is the only way she has of making some pocket money for herself. Go out and bay at the moon if you want. Just leave Sook alone."

Jenny would then hurry out to the back steps to join the rest of the family, who had gathered to watch Sook start her preparations. This was the time of the year when Sook was "the one." She alone knew about the healing qualities of the herbs and roots.

Before Sook blended her various ingredients together, she would inspect them carefully. She would line up her croker sacks full of herbs and roots, then smell and pinch each item before she accepted it. Her discards went into the fire.

Little Bit would shake her head and ask, "Miz Nanny, why you burn dem roots? Ain't dat a gawd-awful sin to waste dem?"

"No," Sook would patiently explain. "If a root is

not firm and crisp, it has lost its power. My medicine must be powerful if it is to sap all that water out of a person's body. My medicine must be as black as the night and as strong as the devil to work."

After the fire was roaring and the water boiling, Sook would start adding the herbs, roots, and other ingredients. She had about ten croker sacks lined up nearby. She would dart from sack to sack, pulling out what she needed and adding it to the big iron pot. The only person who was allowed to help her was Truman. Sook would boil the mixture furiously the first day and then let it simmer the second day. She would constantly skim a disgusting black scum off the top, straining and recooking the entire mixture several times. By the end of the fourth day the mixture would be coal black and putrid. The odor of that foul-smelling brew would permeate the neighborhood. Everyone on the street always knew when it was Miss Nanny's medicine-making time.

After the brew had cooled, Sook would pour the black, cloudy liquid into pint-sized Mason jars and sell them for two dollars each. She had a loyal clientele, including blacks and poor white sharecroppers, who traveled to our house from the distant corners of the county to buy her medicine. Sook always did a thriving business. At one point Jenny even tried unsuccessfully to get a patent for it. Finally, some local doctors started a petition and forced Sook to stop practicing medicine. She made her last batch of dropsy medicine in 1932 when she was sixty-one years old. By then I think she was ready to give up her "hankering" for making medicine.

*~+ *~+ *~+

The centerpiece of *The Grass Harp* is, of course, the tree house—not just any tree house but a true wonder to behold: "spacious, sturdy, a model of a tree house, it was like a raft floating in a sea of leaves." Dolly, Catherine, and Collin, the main characters, find happiness living there for a short time, surely the dream of many a child, living together in a harmonious community.

Truman had his own tree house in the large backyard of Jenny's house. It was always a favorite spot during his lengthy stays with us. By 1929 his parents had started talking about getting a divorce (a scandal that no Faulk had ever fallen into before). In New Orleans Lillie Mae would board a bus with her son and make the journey to Monroeville. There she would deposit her son with us before heading back that next day to join her husband in the hotel room they called home. Even though the impending divorce was sad news for some, to Sook it meant the joy and possession of this sad, grown-up child.

At the start of each visit Truman would make a careful inspection tour of the big house, going from room to room like a bird escaped from its cage. The white serge suit had to go, so he would change into a pair of khaki shorts. If it was barefoot weather, then he would shed his tan-and-white shoes. And then he would head into the backyard and check out his beloved tree house.

A few minutes later, Nelle Harper Lee, Hutch, Billy Eugene, and a couple of other neighborhood children would join Truman in the big backyard. Now their gang was complete. The next few days would be spent making plans for the summer. The tree house would be cleaned and reorganized, bottles would be collected for their lightning bugs, grasshoppers, and June bugs, and magazines would be piled up to await a rainy day when, scissors in hand, they would go through looking for the right pictures to decorate their kites. Summer would be in full swing. Once again Truman had the security of the big white house.

Sook was the first to come up with the idea for a tree house. She wanted a private place apart from the house where she and Truman could spend long hours together away from the rest of the family.

Jenny undertook the construction of the tree house in early 1930. She hoped that by humoring Sook she would get the secret list of ingredients for her dropsy medicine, which she wanted to sell to a manufacturer. (Jenny never did. Sook took her secret recipe with her to the grave.) Truman was six at the time. Jenny selected an eighty-foot-tall black walnut tree that dominated our backyard. This stately tree produced a rich crop of wonderfully oily nuts that we gathered each fall. Its trunk was sixty inches around, and the spreading branches were perfect for the tree house.

"Sook, we have to do this right," Jenny insisted to her sister. "We can't make this tree house with just any wood, which will rot. It has to be cypress. That way it will last for many years."

The building of the tree house became a great

event in our neighborhood. Jenny engaged Frank Salter, a fine carpenter and the husband of my sister Mary Faulk. The first thing he did was saw off the lower limbs of the tree, saying the tree house had to be at least twelve feet above the ground. He also needed large, strong limbs to hold it safely in place. He built a fine structure from cypress wood that circled the thick trunk. Where no branch was available, Frank installed a supporting beam that rose up from the yard. Finally, he added a tin roof, so that Truman and Sook could use their retreat when it rained.

Soon the question arose as to how Sook, Truman, and his young friends would get up and down from the tree house. Sook wanted a spiral staircase, but Jenny insisted that would be much too expensive. Surprisingly, Sook won out. Jenny ending up buying a handsome, antique staircase from a dealer in New Orleans. Once Frank had installed it, the staircase added an elegant touch to the tree house.

Poor Jenny. She never was allowed to visit the tree house once the construction had been completed and Truman and Sook had moved in. It became a haven for the two of them and Truman's young friends from the neighborhood. Inside there was plenty of room for a table and a rattan sofa. They even scattered pillows on the floor to sit on.

Years later Truman would complain to me about how hard it was for him to endure reality. "Reality is so boring," he would say. I think the tree house gave the young Tru a means of escaping from the unpleasant reality of his parents' marital problems. Inside with Sook and his friends he could slip into a fantasy life far away from the harsh realities of the world at large.

4
Children on Their Birthdays

~~~~~~
~~~~~~

C hildren on Their Birthdays" is not one of Truman's better known stories, but it was always one of his own personal favorites. He wrote much of it during a stay in Rome in the summer of 1949. On August 7, by the time he and the playwright Tennessee Williams sailed back together to New York on the *Queen Mary*, he had finished his story. But the event that inspired him took place in the small Southern town of Dallas, North Carolina, in the summer of 1947 when he came to see us for a lengthy visit.

The story has one of Truman's most memorable openings:

Yesterday afternoon the six o'clock bus ran over Miss Bobbit. I'm not sure what there is to be said about it; after all, she was only ten years old, still I know no one of us in this town will forget her. For one thing, nothing she ever did was ordinary, not from the first time that we saw her, and that was a year ago.

I think one reason why Truman was so fond of this story is that his character Miss Lily Jane Bobbit from Memphis, Tennessee, was a kindred spirit of his later creation, Holly Golightly in *Breakfast at Tiffany's*. They are both unattached, unconventional wanderers, dreamers in pursuit of some ideal of happiness. Holly's aim was to have breakfast at Tiffany's. Miss Bobbit puts her dream this way: "Not that I live here, not exactly. I think always about somewhere else, somewhere else where everything is dancing, like children on their birthdays."

Although Miss Bobbit lives in the community only a year, she has a profound effect upon all who meet her. And the fact that she dies at the height of her hopes and desires, unspoiled by disappointments and failures, seems to make her ageless, unspoiled by time and experience.

In 1945 my son Jim was born in New York City. At the time my husband Jimmy and I had an apartment on Gramercy Park. His birth marked both a new beginning for our family and a new business venture between my husband and Joe Capote, my sister's husband. This was to blossom into a highly profitable textile business.

We decided we did not want to bring up our child in New York City, so my husband Jim purchased the original Rudisill residence in the small town of Dallas, North Carolina, not far from Charlotte and nestled in the Blue Ridge Mountains.

My final days in New York were full of happy visits with Truman. He had been living in New York with his mother since 1931. We had become constant companions. He was twenty-one years old at the time. When I returned from work, I often found him sitting on the front steps of our apartment building. On weekends we often had lunch at Schraff's and then took in a movie. At that time Truman clung tenaciously to me. His mother's drinking had made his life so miserable that he had trouble getting any writing done. And he had few friends.

Our apartment on the third floor overlooked a little private park. Truman loved to stand at the window and stare at the sky beyond. I remember one conversation we had before my departure for Dallas.

"Tiny," he said to me, "what does that cloud way over there look like to you?"

I studied it for a moment and then offered that to me it looked like an old man with a long, flowing beard.

"Don't talk like a looney bird, that's not what it looks like." ("Looney" was always one of Truman's favorite words. He used it frequently in his early writings.)

"Well, then, what does it say to you?" I asked.

"It is an old, crooked tree with moss trailing down. It is dying."

"Truman, what makes you have such gloomy thoughts?" I protested.

"Darling Tiny, if my thoughts are gloomy, then it is because they are! I am trying so hard to finish my novel *Summer Crossing* (which would later become *The Grass Harp*). But I just can't work in my mother's apartment. She is always carping on me, complaining about how much I have disappointed her. I just can't work there."

"Well, Truman," I told him, "after I get settled in

Dallas, you come on down with Jimmy when he drives down, stay with us, and finish your book."

But before coming to visit me in Dallas, Truman, on the advice of Carson McCullers, moved into Yaddo, a colony of artists and writers near Sarasota Springs. There he found not only peace and quiet, but someone else who would influence his writings. He met a small, quiet, much older man, Newton Arvin. He was a trustee at Yaddo and a prominent literary critic of his day. Soon afterward they became lovers. Newton was old enough to be Truman's father, and he was an unattractive man who carried around a bundle of neuroses. But both were passionate about one another. Their affair would last until February 1949 when Truman announced that he had found another lover.

Truman left Yaddo on July 17, 1947. He was still looking for a place to write. He wanted to finish *Summer Crossing*. My husband Jimmy drove his bright red Pontiac convertible to Dallas from New York City on one of his periodic trips (he was commuting between the two places) and brought Truman along to spend some time in the peace and quiet of this small Southern town.

In many ways Dallas was then a typical Southern town, very much like Monroeville, Alabama. The Rudisill house was quite old and surrounded in summer by an extravagant array of colorful flowers and lush foliage. Truman loved it. Our cook, Cass, a large black woman with round, rolling eyes, Viola, my small son's nurse, and Dub, our yard man, all made him welcome. From the first he held them captive with his wild, imaginative tales.

Soon Truman had relaxed enough to allow himself to write. He worked on both *Other Voices, Other Rooms* and a short story, "The Headless Hawk." He made good progress and was quite pleased with himself.

One afternoon Truman took time off from his writing to accompany Dub to the old cottonwood tree in the far pasture. Wielding an ax, Dub chopped away part of the tree's trunk to expose a hollow filled with pounds of dark comb honey our bees had gathered from countless thousands of wild blossoms. Truman used to say later that he had never eaten honey as fine as that he and Dub found that afternoon long ago in Dallas.

When he wasn't writing, Truman and I enjoyed lengthy chats. Sometimes he talked about his distress over his mother's growing drinking problem. But more often we discussed the happy memories of our years in Monroeville.

☙ ☙ ☙

I have always thought it strange how many of our happiest memories are usually made up of common things, and those things are often tied up with food. A house filled with the smells of good cooking is one of the things all of us remember from our childhoods, from the world we grew up in. Memories of food, all our deepest memories, are like musical phrases in an intricate symphony; they come in modestly, swell in importance, fade into oblivion, and later return, often livelier than they were before. For example, Truman especially loved and remembered Sook's lemon meringue pie and her Christmas fruitcakes.

I had saved all of Sook's recipes, which had come down from an earlier generation of our family. Truman loved looking through them. Many of them had annotations in Sook's handwriting; some of the sheets of paper were so old they almost disintegrated in our hands. We decided to create a cookbook from the recipes. It was our hope that such a book would evoke the memories that many Southerners share with our family; indeed, many people everywhere who love the old ways and the foods and stories that were so much a part of them.

Truman was eager to have such a cookbook published as a tribute to his beloved Sook. He especially wanted her fruitcake recipes to appear in print. But when Truman skyrocketed to national fame in 1948 after the publication of *Other Voices, Other Rooms*, the cookbook was pushed aside. (In 1972 Truman came to visit me in Charlotte, North Carolina, and we did extensive work on the project we had begun so long ago. By this time I had written a great deal about the characters in the Faulk household—Jenny, Sook, Callie, and Bud; the cook, Little Bit; Corrie, the housekeeper; and the others. After that 1972 visit, I continued working on the cookbook, sometimes consulting by telephone with my nephew. *Sook's Cookbook* was finally published in 1989, a long-overdue tribute to Sook and the way of life that her recipes embody and also to Truman, who so loved that life.)

Truman seemed very nostalgic throughout his 1947 visit to Dallas. Toward the end of his time with us he suddenly showed up in our kitchen and gave me a 7,500-word manuscript.

"What is this, Truman?" I asked.

"It's a story I wrote just for you. It's about Bud because I know how much you loved him."

"What do you want me to do with it?"

"Do whatever you please with it. Why, some day I may even become famous."

That evening I read the novella he had titled *I Remember Grandpa*. The story concerned Bobby, a West Virginia boy, who leaves the beauty of the Allegheny Mountains and the security of his beloved grandparents to move, with his parents, into the city, where he can get a good education and where his father can earn a better living. Told in Bobby's voice, the story captures the sadness of leaving all that is home, the excitement of seeing a larger world and the anticipation of a promised surprise from the grandfather. For me, the story reflected both the young Truman's love for his cousin Bud who had urged the child to think of him as a grandfather and Truman's eventual disappointment in family life and its promised joys.

Truman had typed it on his creaky old Underwood typewriter. He used sheets of paper torn from an old plantation journal which I had salvaged from Jenny's store in Monroeville. The story brought back many fond memories of our cousin Bud. I kept it as Truman's most special gift to me and put it in a drawer of my secretary for safe-keeping. Over the years I forgot about it in the hectic pace of raising a family.

Many years later, on August 25, 1984, after Truman's death, I was going through boxes in my attic and discovered the manuscript. I sat there in the shadows and read *I Remember Grandpa* again for the first time in almost forty years. Then it all came back to me again, that day so long ago.

The Rudisill house in Dallas was built on the highest point of the property, overlooking the road. From our front porch we could look both up and down the blacktop road. Truman loved to sit there when a storm developed and watch the black thunderheads roll across the sky and the lightning flash along the horizon, while the thunder roared.

We were there on this porch that late afternoon in August when the dreadful event occurred that eventually inspired "Children on Their Birthdays." A young neighborhood girl, whom I knew only as Miss Marcy, was standing with her mother alongside the road, waiting for the five o'clock bus to Charlotte. The sky had clouded over, and a light rain started to fall. Miss Marcy suddenly left her side of the road and walked slowly across to the other side just as the bus came around Dead Man's Curve and bore down upon her. She never had a chance. As we watched in horror, the bus struck her head on and tossed her body high into the air. She landed at the edge of the road, rolled over several times, and then lay still. She was dead when we got to her. Truman was terribly shaken by her death. It depressed and bothered him for the rest of his visit.

Like the irritating grain of sand inside the oyster that eventually becomes a pearl, the incident of the girl's death beneath a bus on the road below our house in Dallas on that fateful August afternoon was to lodge in Truman's imagination and slowly over the next two years develop into the short story "Children on Their Birthdays."

5

Other Voices, Other Rooms

+~++~++~++~++~++~++~++~++~++~++~++~++~++~++~+
+~++~++~++~++~++~++~++~++~++~++~++~++~++~++~+

Truman was just twenty-three years old when his first novel, *Other Voices, Other Rooms*, was published in 1948 and created a literary sensation. (Other major novels appearing that year included Norman Mailer's *The Naked and the Dead* and Irwin Shaw's *The Young Lions*.) Truman's novel met with mixed reviews but soon gained a foothold on the *New York Times* bestseller list where it remained for nine weeks.

I remember clearly how shocked I was when I received an advance copy of the novel from Truman and saw on the back cover the photograph of the young Truman, sprawled in suggestive elegance across a Victorian couch, his eyes peering out distrustfully beneath a Napoleonic haircut, his fingers delicately spread over a checked vest.

Of course, I had known about the novel in progress for some time. He had been working on the manuscript the summer before when he visited us in Dallas, North Carolina. We had talked at length about his novel, which had given him considerable difficulty. In fact, he had returned to Monroeville for a visit in 1945. He had been unable to write back in New York at his mother's apartment because of her constant nagging about his being a "sissy." His close friend and companion in adventures, Sook, was then seventy-four years old and suffering from cancer. Each day she took large doses of morphine to dull her pain. She died on January 23, 1946.

I think Truman returned to Monroeville to refresh his memory about his childhood years there and revisit the places that had been important to him during his boyhood. But his visit was not all that successful. Jenny, for one, was not happy with Truman's daily schedule. He preferred to do his writing at night and sleep during much of the day. Then he received a letter from his stepfather, Joe Capote, promising to help him financially. So Truman left Monroeville for New Orleans, hoping again to find a haven where he could write his novel. Apparently,

Joe did not send him as much money as Truman hoped, so he returned to New York City.

Much later Truman would admit that his novel was "an attempt to exorcise demons, an unconscious, altogether intuitive attempt, for I was not aware, except for a few incidents and descriptions, of its being in any serious degree autobiographical. Rereading it now, I find such self-deception unpardonable."

Well, I knew from experience that Truman was from a young age a master at both deception and self-deception. And *Other Voices, Other Rooms* certainly reflected those events and people of his childhood in Monroeville. Joel Knox, the thirteen-year-old boy at the center of the book's action, is clearly Truman's portrait of himself at that age—"too pretty, too delicate, and fair-skinned" with a "girlish tenderness," who offended many people's notions of what a "real" boy ought to look and act like. And Joel, like the young Truman, is also a consummate liar, spinning the most outrageous tales at the drop of a hat.

The story line follows the young Joel's journey from New Orleans to Noon City en route to the decaying Southern plantation called Skully's

Landing. There he expects to be reunited with his father, Ed Samsom, who has been absent from Joel's life for the past twelve years. Soon after the death of his divorced mother a short time before, he had received a letter, ostensibly written by his father, asking him to come to the Landing. The journey there is marked by a gradual shift away from the real and familiar toward the unreal and grotesque. At Skully's Landing, he learns that his father is a mute paraplegic. He finds himself virtually a prisoner at the hands of his cousin, Randolph, who had, in actual fact, written Joel's letter of invitation. The final stage of Joel's journey is a trip with Randolph through the swamp to the mysterious and dilapidated Cloud Hotel, where the young boy finally accepts his situation, which includes becoming the lover of his cousin Randolph. Critics were quick to comment on the novel's atmosphere of isolation and decadence, which placed it firmly within the tradition of Southern Gothic fiction.

I was shocked but not surprised to see how many of the events and people from Truman's years with Jenny and the rest of us had ended up in his first novel. He had clearly created *Other Voices, Other Rooms* out of the prevailing patterns of his early years. And certainly his father Archie was never really there for his son, a fact that clearly had disturbed the young Truman.

~+ ~+ ~+

The first and most obvious parallel is the character of Idabel, who becomes Joel's friend during his early months at the Landing. She is so much a tomboy that she reminds Joel of "a beefy little roughneck" he had known in New Orleans. Her character is clearly based on Truman's closest friend in Monroeville, Nelle Harper Lee, who lived next door. They were constant companions and always into mischief together. The pair of them probably flew more kites, played more games of jacks, shot more marbles, and shinnied up more trees than any two authors in the world. Nelle's character Dill Harris in *To Kill a Mockingbird* is a faithful portrait of the young Truman. And Truman, in turn, took Nelle's tomboyish qualities and exaggerated them for *Other Voices, Other Rooms*.

Born in Monroeville on April 28, 1926, Nelle was two years younger than Truman. Although both shared the same rich texture of life in a small town, Nelle had the added benefit of parents who were loving and caring toward her. Her father, Amasa Coleman Lee, came to Monroeville in 1913 and went to work as a legal apprentice in the law firm of Barnett and Bugg. Two years later Mr. Lee was admitted to the bar, and in 1916 he became a partner with Barnett and Bugg. From 1929 to 1947 he served as the editor of our local weekly newspaper, the *Monroeville Journal*. The portrait of Atticus Finch in *To Kill a Mockingbird* is an idealization of Nelle's father. (There never was any such trial, by the way, at least not in Monroeville, and Mr. Lee never handled any cases that were remotely like that in Nelle's novel.)

Truman did not spend much time in Nelle's house; she always came to our place. The Lee house was different, much more subdued. Truman and Nelle had much more freedom at our place. Jenny was away during the day. There was always something to eat. She and Truman loved to walk along the top of the backyard fence or play in the tree house. When they were not in the tree house, with its collection of old magazines and glass jars full of grasshoppers and butterflies, the chances were they would be under the big yellow rosebushes in the backyard with an ancient Underwood typewriter that Mr. Lee had given them. They loved to play at being writers. Nelle would drag the big Underwood over. Truman would bring his tattered copy of Webster's Dictionary. Together they would sit for hours, pecking away.

Their time together was precious to the young Truman. For the twentieth-anniversary edition of *Other Voices, Other Rooms*, he wrote a lengthy preface in which he recalled fondly, "Idabel, or rather the girl who was the counterpart of Idabel, and how we used to wade and swim in the pure waters [at Hatter's Mill], where fat speckled fish lolled in sunlit pools; [and she] was always trying to reach out and grab one."

Truman and Nelle remained best buddies long after he left Monroeville.

Their lives became closely intermeshed years later when she accompanied him west to Holcomb, Kansas, on the first two of his fact-finding expeditions for *In Cold Blood*, his non-fiction novel about the impact of a monstrous multiple murder upon a small, isolated farm community. When Random House published the novel in 1966, it carried Truman's dedication to Nelle in grateful appreciation of her support and assistance.

✢✢ ✢✢ ✢✢

Another character in *Other Voices, Other Rooms*, who had been suggested by a member of our household was Missouri Fever, the black cook at Skully's Landing. Truman described her:

> "Tall, powerful, barefoot, graceful, soundless, Missouri Fever was like a supple black cat as she paraded serenely about the kitchen, the casual flow of her walk beautifully sensuous and haughty. . . . The length of her neck was something to ponder upon, for she was almost a freak, a human giraffe. . . . A narrow scar circled her neck like a necklace of purple wire."

In Jenny's household we had Corrie, our house servant, and Little Bit, our cook, both of whom had lived on the premises for as long as I could remember. They had started working for Jenny shortly after she built her store and big house at the turn of the century. By the time I moved in, they were every bit as much a part of the household as Bud, Sook, and

Callie. I don't know what Jenny paid them—probably no more than five dollars a week, if that. But she took care of all their needs, and whatever clothes they wanted they got free from her store.

Little Bit was a woman with the agility and cunning of a Siamese cat. She was part Cajun, part Indian, and part Negro. Or, as she boasted, "Just a li'l bit of everything." A deep scar ran across her left cheek from the tip of her ear to her chin. As unsightly as it was, the livid scar did not detract that much from her oval-shaped cameo face, accentuated by long black hair parted in the middle and combed over her temples to conceal all of the ears except the tips of her lobes. For so slender a face her mouth was startling full and red-lipped. Little Bit was really quite a handsome woman. She did not know her age. "I'se figures I'se about Miz Jenny's age, more or less," she would say thoughtfully. "But I'se cant's be certain. Ain't nobody kept no records on birthin' of blacks in dose days."

Little Bit's love for men was no secret. At the drop of a hat she would say, "Dere's no sweeter place to lay for love dan in a fresh haymow. Gawd, jist smellin' dat mixture of horse an' hay is purely like bitin' into unexpected pepper." When we asked her why she always made love in an enclosed barn, Little Bit would shake her head and answer, "De ground always looks shaky in de moonlight. I'se fearful of de long branches of dose trees. Dey goin' reach right down an' pull me up to Gawd knows where. More dan likely plat-eyes an' spirits run round de ground. De ground ain't no place to take yore lover at night!"

Little Bit lived in the house in a small bedroom just off our kitchen. She had her hands full just feeding our household. She was an excellent cook. "Lord," Bud would say when Little Bit had one of his favorite dishes cooking away on her stove, "people gnaw their fingers and bite their tongues just to get a smell of the steam when she raises them pot lids!"

※ ※ ※

In Truman's novel, Missouri Fever's father is Jesus Fever, an ancient black man who over seventy years before had been a slave on the Skully's Landing plantation. His proudest possession is a sword used in the Civil War. He brings it out on the occasion of Joel's visit to his cabin, and they admire it together.

Truman describes it as "a beautiful sword with a silver handle: across the blade there was inscribed, *Unsheath Me Not Without Reason—Sheath Me Not Without Honor.*" Jesus Fever tells the boy that Randolph's grandfather had given him the sword over sixty years before.

Our cousin Bud, the only man living at Jenny's house, had just such a sword hanging on the wall of his bedroom. I remember one afternoon when Truman and I sat in Bud's room, chatting. Tru suddenly pointed to the sword and asked, "Bud, where did you get the Confederate sword hanging there on your wall?"

Bud gave a squirt of tobacco into a spittoon in a corner near his bed and settled down for a story.

"That sword belonged to William, my father. He enlisted on April 10, 1862, in the Thirty-sixth Alabama, Confederacy, Company F. He was a brave warrior and fought in many engagements. He was finally wounded at the Battle of Shiloh. Took one bullet through his back and another creased his knee."

"Was that a bad war?" Truman asked.

"Yes, Truman," Bud said slowly, "that was a bad war. And I don't want to talk about it.

Bud waited a spell and then continued.

"My father came home all broken up. People say he died spiritually on the day Lee surrendered his sword at Appomattox. His land had been pilfered, his slaves turned loose, and he had no money. This was probably the doings of scalawags, but he put the blame on Sherman. William worked hard on his plantation for ten years and then just gave up. He spent the last years of his life rocking on the front porch and damning the Yankees. His war injuries hurt him all his life, and he took morphine to kill the pain. Sometimes he took too much and became dependent upon it."

In 1952 Jenny's big house in Monroeville burned down. Jenny, Sook, Carrie, and Bud were all dead by then, but William's sword still hung in its place of honor on Bud's wall. It was destroyed in the fire.

⚬ ⚬ ⚬

Truman's Miss Amy, Joel's father's second wife, is a shrewish woman who makes clear from the start that she has no love for the young Joel and no desire for him to settle in at Skully's Landing. The young boy meets her for the first time when he awakes in his bedroom at the Landing and discovers Miss Amy, poker in hand, in his room chasing a blue jay that had gotten trapped inside. "Her dress was of an almost transparent grey material," he wrote. "On her left hand, for no clear reason, she wore a matching grey silk glove, and she kept the hand cupped daintily, as if it were crippled."

Truman clearly based the character of Miss Amy on another member of our household in Monroeville, Jenny's younger sister Callie. Her fate, her burden in life, was not to be able to escape Jenny. They were bound together for life in a strange dependence that ate at both of them. Jenny hated her sister for her weakness. Callie hated Jenny for her strength. Every effort by Callie to establish some sort of life independent of Jenny was deliberately frustrated.

When Callie was eighteen years old, she began to teach school. She had acquired a teacher's certificate from a "normal" school. In those days professional requirements for teachers were virtually nonexistent. Callie went to work in a one-room rural schoolhouse near Franklin, Alabama, teaching several grades and all subjects.

There was too little love in Callie for her ever to have been a good teacher. The parents of the children hated her. Callie did mean things sometimes, such as sending her dirtier pupils home to their parents (probably poor white sharecroppers) with neatly printed signs around their necks that read, "Wash this boy's ears. They have enough dirt in them to grow corn!"

When Lillie Mae brought her infant son to Jenny's house to stay shortly after his birth, Callie welcomed him in a cool, restrained way. In sharp contrast, Sook and Bud were delighted to have him there. Callie never mistreated the young Truman, but he always knew that she merely tolerated him.

But Truman also drew on his grandmother, Mabel Knox, for one important detail of the character of Amy. Mabel was a lovely aristocratic woman from Troy, Alabama. Like Amy, she always wore a glove on her left hand. We never knew what had happened to her hand. None of us dared ask her. It always remained a mystery. And her maiden name was Knox. That was the family name Truman gave Joel.

✦✦✦ ✦✦✦ ✦✦✦

Joel and Randolph end up at the Cloud Hotel deep in the forest on the edge of the Drowning Pool.

Years before the place had been popular with crowds of prosperous vacationers in elegant attire. But at the time of Joel's visit it sits empty and abandoned, looked after only by Little Sunshine, an aging black man. "The hotel rose before them like a mound of bones," Truman wrote in his novel. "Swan stairs soft with mildewed carpet curved upward from the hotel's lobby; the diabolic tongue of a cuckoo bird, protruding out of a wall-clock, mutely proclaimed an hour forty years before, and on the room clerk's splintery desk stood dehydrated specimens of potted palms."

The Cloud Hotel, too, is based on fact. It was a spooky place that Truman loved to visit when looking for a scary adventure. This was the old Robbins Hotel, a crumbling two-story building with fourteen bedrooms, each with a fireplace, which stood abandoned and forlorn in the middle of some woods a good distance from Monroeville. Owned and operated by Miss Minnie Robbins, it was known to us folks around town as the "hotel nobody ran." After Miss Minnie's retirement, the old hotel stood as a startling monument of public trust and faith in strangers. The place became popular with visiting hunters and fisherman. A book for signatures of guests was placed on a small table in the front hallway under a sign that read, "Leave your dollars on the bed when you check out." This the guests did faithfully after consulting a note fixed to the wall by their room's door to see if they had occupied a $2.50 or a $3.00 room. Only one faithful servant remained on duty, an aged black man.

On several occasions I accompanied Truman and Sook to see Miss Minnie at her hotel during the Christmas season. She always visited there at that time of year to serve fruitcake and coffee to the hunters staying in her hotel. We regarded her as one of Monroeville's finest cooks. In fact, she gave Sook one of her recipes for fruitcake. Miss Minnie lived to be ninety-nine years old.

✳ ✳ ✳

And, finally, there is one character people are always asking me about, cousin Randolph, who loves to dress up in a white wedding dress and position himself in his bedroom window. That character is almost entirely a creature of Truman's imagination. But at a distance behind Randolph stands the figure of

Truman's cousin Bud Faulk. For it was Bud who first introduced the young Truman to homosexuality. I did not mention this important fact in my first book because I wanted to protect Bud's reputation. But he died a good many years ago, and I now think that the record should be set straight.

The fact is that Bud never had any interest in women. He was the only man in our town who never noticed a well-attired woman if she walked past him. On several occasions Jenny invited eligible single women around to the house for the express purpose of meeting her brother. But Bud never showed any interest. Several of us back then suspected that Bud liked men, especially young boys, better than the opposite sex.

Jenny would get upset whenever Truman went into Bud's room. He had a big antique four-poster bed in there with a soft feather mattress that felt just like lying on a cloud. The young Truman loved to play on top of Bud's bed. And the two of them would often lie on top of the bed together, much to Jenny's distress. She tolerated that behavior as long as Bud kept the door to his bedroom open. But if he closed the door, Jenny would fly into a rage and rush up, pound on his door, and demand, "Bud, you keep this door open when Truman is in there, or you'll have to account to me!"

Bud did something else with Truman that made Jenny nervous. Bud loved to sit on the swing on our front porch and glide back and forth for hours on end. If Truman was about, then Bud would seat the youngster on his lap. The two of them would swing contentedly for long periods of time, while Jenny would about have a fit.

Another thing about Bud that later made me suspicious about him was that he and his younger brother Howard never spoke. Jenny often invited Howard to join us for Sunday dinner. He always chose to sit at the opposite end of the table from Bud. They always went through the entire dinner without exchanging so much as a single word. To my knowledge the brothers never spoke to one another throughout their adult lives. My sense was that some dark secret kept them apart.

Truman always had enormous affection for his cousin Bud. His influence on the boy may not have been as tangible as Sook's, but it was real and lasting. And Bud strongly believed that some day Truman would surprise everyone and become a big success. I remember when Truman left us in 1930 to live with his mother in New York City. Bud put his big, liver-spotted hand gently on Truman's head and murmured, "This boy has been blessed by God's grace. I've always felt, Truman, that someday you will be famous. I know that I will never live to see it, but others in the family will."

Epilogue

In the summer of 1930 Lillie Mae, then twenty-five, saw a notice in the *Mobile Register* for an Elizabeth Arden beauty contest and entered her picture. She won first prize, which consisted of a trip to New York City and a free beauty course. Some weeks after arriving in the city, she wrote her husband, Arch, in New Orleans and informed him that she would not be returning and wanted a divorce. Arch was crushed, but he did not contest the divorce.

Within a few months, Lillie Mae landed a job as the manager of the Green Line Restaurant near Wall Street. The busy restaurant specialized in Southern cooking, and it was famous for its chicken pot pie, fresh strawberry pie, hot sourdough rolls, and three small pots of fresh fruit preserves on each table.

Soon after starting work at the Green Line, Lillie Mae met Joe Capote, who quickly fell for her. He told her he was a Cuban millionaire. Joe *was* Cuban, but he was far from being a millionaire. He was a controller at Taylor, Pinkham and Company. He did make a fair amount of money, but he spent it as though he had a great deal more and moved in a fast, stylish circle of socially prominent people. Lillie Mae decided on their first date that she would marry him.

Eventually, Joe set Lillie Mae up in a large apartment. Soon after that, she asked me to bring Truman up to New York. We left by train in the early part of September 1931, and I moved in with my sister. She had the front bedroom, while Truman and I shared the one in the back of the apartment. When Lillie Mae and Joe married in 1937, they moved to Greenwich, Connecticut, taking Truman with them.

*   *

After leaving Monroeville and the South, Truman followed a path that took him farther and farther away from his childhood memories. Although his links with the past faded as the years progressed, there are traces of his early memories and experiences throughout his writings. It is my hope that this book will give readers a reason to rediscover

Truman's work and perhaps a deeper appreciation of it after learning the origins of some of his ideas and stories.

In the final months of his life, Truman was returning both spiritually and creatively to his Southern roots. The memories of his happy times under Jenny's roof—the big Christmas dinners, Sook's medicine making, the smells of Little Bit's kitchen, and the endless stream of Tom Sawyer–esque adventures in and around Monroeville—haunted Truman throughout his life.

About the Authors

Marie Rudisill is an established author with four books and hundreds of newspaper and magazine articles to her credit. She was for many years a dealer of antiques and wrote numerous articles on the subject for a variety of magazines, including *Antiques*. For six years she was the antiques editor at the *Raleigh* (North Carolina) *News* and wrote a weekly column on the topic that was syndicated by the Frank Daniels chain of newspapers. In 1998 the University of Mississippi Press named Mrs. Rudisill one of the South's top writers of Southern cookbooks. She currently lives in Hudson, Florida.

James C. Simmons is the author of thirteen books and over five hundred magazine articles on travel, history, and wildlife. Raised in Cincinnati, he received his bachelor's degree from Miami University in Oxford, Ohio, and a doctorate in nineteenth-century British literature from the University of California at Berkeley. Before becoming a freelance writer, he taught courses on British and American literature at Boston University and San Diego State University, including seminars on Southern regional novels. His book *Americans: The View from Abroad* won first prize as Best Travel Book of 1990 in the Lowell Thomas Competition of Travel Journalism. He also writes privately commissioned life, family, and corporate histories. He lives in San Diego. Please visit his Web site at *www.yourbiography.com.*